D1049036

Celebrating
Mercy

Celebrating Mercy

PONTIFICAL COUNCIL FOR THE PROMOTION
OF THE NEW EVANGELIZATION

Jubilee of Mercy
2015-2016

Our Sunday Visitor Publishing Division
Our Sunday Visitor, Inc.
Huntington, Indiana 46750

Scripture texts in this work are taken from the *New American Bible, revised edition* © 2010, 1991, 1986, 1970 Confraternity of Christian Doctrine, Washington, D.C., and are used by permission of the copyright owner. All rights reserved. No part of the *New American Bible* may be reproduced in any form without permission in writing from the copyright owner.

Excerpts from the English translation of *The Roman Missal* © 2010, International Commission on English in the Liturgy Corporation (ICEL). All rights reserved.

Copyright © 2015 Pontifical Council for the Promotion of the New Evangelization Vatican City

Published 2015 by Our Sunday Visitor Publishing Division

20 19 18 17 16 15   1 2 3 4 5 6 7 8 9

All rights reserved. With the exception of short excerpts for critical reviews, no part of this work may be reproduced or transmitted in any form or by any means whatsoever without permission from the publisher. For more information, visit: www.osv.com/permissions

Our Sunday Visitor Publishing Division, Our Sunday Visitor, Inc., 200 Noll Plaza, Huntington, IN 46750; 1-800-348-2440

ISBN: 978-1-61278-975-0 (Inventory No. T1735)
eISBN: 978-1-61278-983-5
LCCN: 2015949828

Translation: Monsignor Daniel Gallagher
Cover design: Lindsey Riesen
Cover art: Shutterstock; Pontifical Council for the Promotion of the New Evangelization
Interior design: Sherri Hoffman

PRINTED IN THE UNITED STATES OF AMERICA

TABLE OF CONTENTS

FOREWORD

"We constantly need to contemplate the mystery of mercy. It is a wellspring of joy, serenity, and peace. Our salvation depends on it." Pope Francis could not have chosen more fitting words to express the value of mercy in the Church's life and the lives of all believers. To contemplate mercy means to see it imprinted on the very face of Christ, who lives and is really present in the mystery of the holy Eucharist. Every time the Church celebrates the sacraments, she does nothing but bring the Father's mercy alive, making it present as he acts through his Son and converts hearts steeped in violence, transforming sacramental matter into a source of efficient grace for our salvation. It is the work of the Holy Spirit and the transforming power of his action that strengthens anything that is weak within us.

Above all else, the Jubilee of Mercy needs to be celebrated. The symbolic words and rituals that make it up culminate in the liturgical celebration by which the whole Church prays and intensely lives the mystery of her existence as communion. Among the other pastoral guidebooks in this series aimed at helping the faithful live this extraordinary Jubilee, this volume, entitled *Celebrating Mercy*, occupies a special place. The Pontifical Council for the Promotion of the New Evangelization is particularly grateful to Father Silvano M. Maggiani, O.S.M., for putting together the various parts of this pastoral guide. We would also like to acknowledge Father Pietro Angelo Muroni and Monsignor Angelo Lameri for their valuable professional assistance in bringing this guidebook to light.

We have no doubt that by reflecting on these guidelines for the

Holy Year and adapting them to local ecclesial and cultural situations, the faithful will discover a wealth of possibilities for actively engaging in the celebration of the Jubilee of Mercy. By celebrating mercy, the faithful will more effectively live it and give witness to it as a reflection of the Father's mercy.

✠ Rino Fisichella
President, Pontifical Council for the
Promotion of the New Evangelization

INTRODUCTION

Many kinds of jubilees have been celebrated throughout the history of the Church at the invitation of various popes. Among the rituals making up a Jubilee, including more recent ones, liturgical celebrations hold pride of place both in the Church of Rome, presided over by her bishop, the pope, and in the universal Church, manifested in individual dioceses throughout the world guided by their pastors, the bishops. It is in this spirit of universality and collegiality that Pope Francis, in his Bull of Indiction announcing the extraordinary Jubilee of Mercy, *Misericordiae Vultus*, decreed that the ritual opening of the Holy Door of Mercy in the Basilica of St. Peter would take place on December 8, 2015, the solemnity of the Immaculate Conception. That will mark the official opening of the Holy Year. Then, on December 13, the Third Sunday of Advent, "in every local church, at the cathedral — the mother church of the faithful in any particular area — or, alternatively, at the co-cathedral or another church of special significance, a Door of Mercy will be opened for the duration of the Holy Year. At the discretion of the local ordinary, a similar door may be opened at any shrine frequented by large groups of pilgrims, since visits to these holy sites are so often grace-filled moments, as people discover a path to conversion. Every Particular Church, therefore, will be directly involved in living out this Holy Year as an extraordinary moment of grace and spiritual renewal. Thus the Jubilee will be celebrated both in Rome and in the Particular Churches as a visible sign of the Church's universal communion" (*Misericordiae Vultus*, 3).

From that moment, which will mark the solemn beginning of the Holy Year in each and every diocese, particular churches and local communities will see to it that the Jubilee is lived, particularly through the liturgy, "as an extraordinary moment of grace and spiritual renewal" (*Misericordiae Vultus*, 3) by all the People of God. This indeed will be the case if there is a large-scale commitment to promoting Jubilee celebrations that, in their unique character, simplicity and beauty — and within the context of the liturgical cycle for Year C — there is a clear, mystogogical manifestation of the merciful love and care of the heavenly Father who, with the Son and through the work of the Holy Spirit, "desires all men to be saved and to come to the knowledge of the truth" (1 Tm 2:4).

In *Misericordiae Vultus*, Pope Francis recalls that there are times when "we are called to gaze even more attentively on mercy so that we may become a more effective sign of the Father's action in our lives" (3). The liturgy is a privileged moment when we can recognize and allow ourselves to marvel at the Father's merciful gaze.

This liturgical aid is intended as a tool for all diocesan and religious communities, parishes, and shrines, so that they can devise and implement ways to celebrate the Jubilee so that it may be filled with the sweet smelling fragrance of the Father's mercy.

CHAPTER ONE

The Liturgical Year

Since the liturgical year is the hinge upon which the entire pastoral and liturgical activity of the Church will turn during the Jubilee Year, it should be given pride of place in each and every community by careful attention to the quality of liturgical celebrations (see *Sacrosanctum Concilium*, 102). Special celebrations during the Jubilee Year should always be carried out in harmony with the readings of Year C in the liturgical cycle, which coincides with the extraordinary Jubilee. Of particular importance will be Sunday, the Lord's Day, when the Church celebrates the mystery of Christ's death and resurrection, as well as the Christmas and Easter cycles. In addition to the liturgical celebration, "Sunday should also give the faithful an opportunity to devote themselves to works of mercy, charity, and the apostolate. To experience the joy of the Risen Lord deep within is to share fully the love which pulses in his heart: there is no joy without love! Jesus himself explains this, linking the 'new commandment' with the gift of joy: 'If you keep my commandments, you will remain in my love, just as I have kept the Father's commandments and remain in his love. I have told you this that my own joy may be in you and your joy may be complete. This is my commandment: that you love one another as I have loved you' (Jn 15:10-12)" (Pope John Paul II, *Dies Domini*, 69).

The Season of Lent

Lent is a privileged time when the Church is called to give even greater witness to the merciful face of the Father, especially in penitential liturgies and in the celebration of the Sacrament of Reconciliation. For this reason, on Friday, March 4, and Saturday, March 5, local communities, and particularly parishes, shrines, and churches more centrally located and/or hosting a larger number of regular visitors, are encouraged to participate in an initiative called "24 hours for the Lord." Similarly, a special penitential liturgy will be celebrated at St. Peter's Basilica in Rome on March 4.

Other events should be privileged during the Lenten season, such as the celebration of the Liturgy of the Word. In this regard, the Holy Father recommends "the season of Lent during this Jubilee Year should also be lived more intensely as a privileged moment to celebrate and experience God's mercy. How many pages of Sacred Scripture are appropriate for meditation during the weeks of Lent to help us rediscover the merciful face of the Father!" (*Misericordiae Vultus*, 17). The booklet entitled *The Parables of Mercy*, published by the Pontifical Council for the Promotion of the New Evangelization, may be of particular help in this regard.

The scriptural readings that occur during the Lenten cycle are there for very specific reasons in that they emphasize the particular themes of this privileged season — namely, baptism and penance. More specifically, the Holy Year of Mercy coincides with Year C of the cycle of readings in the Lectionary: a cycle particularly rich with the theme of penance. Throughout the year, we will be called to walk the path of conversion that leads to Easter, the supreme event of reconciliation with the Father. The homily will play a key role in the liturgies of this season, but no less important will be brief exhortations and the prayers of the faithful by which pastors, together with their collaborators, will help the celebrating assemblies enter into the mystery of the Father's mercy celebrated eminently in the sacrifice of his Son. Helpful in this regard will be the *Homiletic Directory*, recently published by the Vatican's Congregation for Divine Worship and the Discipline of the Sacraments.

In particular, with the reading of Jesus's temptations in the desert on the First Sunday of Lent (Lk 4:1-13), the People of God will be called to live the Lenten season as a journey of "ecclesial conversion" by listening to the Word of God, praying, and fasting. On the Second Sunday of Lent, with the reading of the Transfiguration (Lk 9:28-36), Christians will be invited to root their faith in the mystery of Christ's death and resurrection so that they may adhere, in full fidelity to the Covenant, to God's will and become true disciples of Christ. The parable of the withered fig tree (Lk 13:1-9), read on the Third Sunday of Lent, will encourage the faithful to overcome their hardness of mind and heart so that, welcoming the Word of God and making room for the Spirit, they may bear the fruit of genuine and ongoing conversion. The parable of the merciful father on the Fourth Sunday of Lent (Lk 15:1-3,11-32) will be the culmination of the Lenten journey in this Jubilee Year as the faithful are called to recognize God as the good Father, abundant in mercy, who embraces in love all his children who return to him with a repentant heart, wrapping them in the mantle of salvation and making them partakers of the joy of the eternal Paschal banquet, restoring them to the royal dignity of the children of God. The passage about the adulterous woman (Jn 8:1-11), read on the Fifth Sunday of Lent, calls all the baptized to open themselves completely to the unconditional mercy of God who renews all things in Christ.

This season, especially through the celebration of the Liturgy of the Word, will offer special occasions to reflect on the topic of reconciliation: baptism and penance are the two bedrocks upon which the entire Lenten journey takes place. The *Rite of Christian Initiation for Adults* also designates Lent as a time of "purification and enlightenment" (21), since in "the liturgy and liturgical catechesis of Lent the reminder of baptism already received or the preparation for its reception, as well as the theme of repentance, renew the entire community along with those being prepared to celebrate the paschal mystery, in which each of the elect will share through the sacraments of initiation" (125).

Thus, before the celebration of "election," the catechumens are required to make a conversion, but in mind and in their way of life, in addition to having a sufficient knowledge of Christian doctrine and an active sense of faith and charity. Moreover, "this is a period of more intense spiritual preparation, consisting more in interior reflection than in catechetical instruction, and is intended to purify the minds and hearts of the elect as they search their own consciences and do penance. This period is intended as well to enlighten the minds and hearts of the elect with a deeper knowledge of Christ the Savior. All of this is brought about through the celebration of certain rites, especially the scrutinies and the presentations" (126). Special care should be given to these rites; may they be "a sign of the Church's maternal solicitude for the People of God, enabling them to enter the profound richness of this mystery so fundamental to the faith" (*Misericordiae Vultus*, 18).

Holy Week and Easter Time

The celebration of Holy Week, and especially of the Easter Triduum, must also be prepared carefully during this Jubilee Year. Indeed, the liturgical language used in these ceremonies, consisting of the words, signs, symbols, and gestures proper to them, especially the veneration of the cross on Good Friday, makes visible the mystery of the love and the justification of the Father revealed in the sacrifice of his Son for the whole human race. These celebrations culminate in the Easter Vigil, through the history of salvation recounted in the Liturgy of the Word and the celebration of the sacraments that represent the Father's concern for his children. As they celebrate Holy Week and the Easter season, pastors must not fail to reveal the image of the Father who saved us and continues to save us. God showed his mercy toward Israel, his people, and even today he never tires of showing his merciful face to anyone who accepts the gift of faith in the waters of the baptismal font.

The Feast of the Exaltation of the Cross

For centuries, the cross has stood as a symbol of the most horrific kind of punishment, and, in a certain sense, it still does. Indeed, how many Christians, even today, in the name of the Cross of Christ, give their lives in martyrdom! The cross thus stands as a special sign, and all the more should it do so in this Holy Year, especially in lands and churches afflicted by violence and oppression because of their faith in the Crucified and Risen Christ. In fact, for the Christian, the tree of the cross is a grafting of the tree of justice and peace (Christ himself) to the tree of life (the wedding chamber, the throne, the altar of the New Covenant). From Christ, the new Adam asleep on the cross, springs forth the wonderful sacrament of the entire Church. The cross is a sign of Christ's dominion over all who, in baptism, are configured to him in death and glory (see Rom 6:5).

According to the Church Fathers, the cross is a sign of the Son of Man who will appear at the end of time (see Mt 24:29-31), but also a sign of the great mercy of the Father who, for love of mankind, offers his Son as a sacrificial victim for the sins of mankind. For this reason, it stands as the primary symbol of this Holy Year. The feast of the Exaltation of the Cross, which in the East is given a place comparable to that of Easter, deserves to be celebrated with great solemnity as it highlights the mystery of love and redemption which is the cross of Christ: "For you placed the salvation of the human race on the wood of the cross, so that, where death arose, life might again spring forth and the evil one, who conquered on a tree, might likewise on a tree be conquered" (*Preface of the Exaltation of the Holy Cross*).

In each community it is fitting, especially on this feast day and throughout the liturgical year, that, with due respect for liturgical norms, the cross in the presbytery or in the church hall be decorated in such a way that it stands as an eminent sign of God's mercy and Christ's victory over death and, for this reason, remains a reference point for communal prayer and private reflection.

The Solemnity of the Most Sacred Heart of Jesus

On the Friday following the Second Sunday after Pentecost, which occurs on June 3 in this Jubilee Year, the Church celebrates the solemnity of the Most Sacred Heart of Jesus. Taking its inspiration from sacred Scripture, this solemnity summarizes the very mystery of Christ, the totality of his being, his very person considered in his most intimate and essential core: the Son of God, uncreated wisdom; infinite charity, the principle of salvation and sanctification for the entire community.

The "heart of Jesus" is Christ, the Word incarnate and the Savior, intrinsically ordered, in the Spirit, with infinite divine-human love toward the Father and toward us, his brothers and sisters. The "heart of Jesus," therefore, is the seat of the Father's mercy who has opened the infinite treasures of his love and patience toward mankind.

Accordingly, this feast day, which has a wide appeal in popular piety, must be celebrated with particular solemnity in this Holy Year as it calls the People of God to conversion and reparation for sins. It also instills in them love and gratitude to God who guides our hearts in the love and patience of Christ. Finally, it strengthens them in the apostolic mission through consecration to Christ and his salvific work. For this reason, the Congregation for Divine Worship and the Discipline of the Sacraments explain, "the devotion is recommended and its renewal encouraged by the Holy See and by the bishops. Such renewal touches on the devotion's linguistic and iconographic expressions; on consciousness of its biblical origins and its connection with the great mysteries of the faith; on affirming the primacy of the love of God and neighbor as the essential content of the devotion itself" (*Directory on Popular Piety and the Liturgy*, 172).

During this extraordinary Jubilee Year, Pope Francis wishes to entrust all priests to the "Heart of Christ" as we celebrate the 160th anniversary of the institution of this solemnity by Pope Pius IX in 1856. It is opportune for each diocese and community to promote times to pray for priests on this feast day, as priests are the primary ministers of divine mercy but also men who need to experience the mercy of the one and only Father. During the prayers of the faithful at Mass, special intentions should be included for priests, as well as one of the intercessory prayers at both morning and evening prayer on that day. On this day, in the cathedral churches of respective dioceses, prayer vigils should be promoted as well as extended periods of time for Eucharistic Adoration with the explicit intention of the Church's ordained ministers. Both priests and laypersons are invited to take part in these services. For this reason, a convenient time should be chosen to facilitate the participation of both priests and laity.

Special moments of prayer should also be dedicated to men and women belonging to institutes of consecrated life, who are in the midst of celebrating a special Year for Consecrated Life that concludes on February 2, 2016, the feast of the Presentation of the Lord. On this day, it is recommended that the diocesan bishop gather with religious men and women at the cathedral to celebrate the feast of the Presentation of the Lord, which begins with the liturgy of light and recalls in a special way their consecration to God, rich in mercy and abundant in kindness.

CHAPTER TWO

The Celebration of the Sacraments

The specific vocation of pastors and sacred ministers is to make visible, particularly through the celebration of the sacraments and the words and gestures of the liturgy, the Father's mercy and his care for each of his children expressed in the gift of sacramental grace. There are some sacraments, however, in which this aspect emerges more strongly than in others.

Baptism, Reconciliation, and the Anointing of the Sick

Besides the holy Eucharist, special mention should be made of the Sacraments of Baptism, Reconciliation, and the Anointing of the Sick.

In regard to the first, by means of the mystogogical journey clearly visible in the initiatory signs with which the *Rite of Baptism* is richly endowed, care should be taken to emphasize that the baptismal font is the "doorway" to all the sacraments through which one is introduced to the Church's sacramental life and clothed in the image of God that every Christian is called to keep free from the stain of sin for eternal life.

The Sacrament of Reconciliation takes on even greater relevance in the Holy Year of Mercy. Further reflections on the nature and celebration of this sacrament can be found in *Confession: Sacrament of Mercy*, by the Pontifical Council for the Promotion of the New Evangelization.

In the Sacrament of the Anointing of the Sick, administered with particular care to those preparing to leave this world and meet the Father, particular emphasis should be given to the dimension of expectant hope for the beatific vision of the God who has not come to condemn but to forgive.

The Eucharist

The Eucharist, the "source and summit" of the Church's life, is for that reason also the main point of reference for all the celebrations and activities taking place in this extraordinary Holy Year. The Eucharist, in fact, is the centerpiece of the Church's sacramental life and the *consummatio vitae spiritualis et omnium sacramentorum finis* ("the consummation of the spiritual life and the end of all the sacraments"), as St. Thomas Aquinas teaches. It is the culminating point of the mercy received in the Sacrament of Reconciliation through a participation in the body and blood of Christ with the entire community of the baptized. "In the Eucharist Christ gives us the very body which he gave up for us on the cross, the very blood which he 'poured out for many for the forgiveness of sins' [Mt 26:28].... Its memory perpetuated until the end of the world, and its salutary power ... applied to the forgiveness of the sins we daily commit" (*Catechism of the Catholic Church*, 1365-66).

The Sacraments of the Eucharist and Penance are closely interconnected. St. John Paul II explained in his encyclical *Ecclesia de Eucharistia*: "Because the Eucharist makes present the redeeming sacrifice of the Cross, perpetuating it sacramentally, it naturally gives rise to a continuous need for conversion, for a personal response to the appeal made by St. Paul to the Christians in Corinth: 'We beseech you on behalf of Christ, be reconciled to God' (2 Cor 5:20). If a Christian's conscience is burdened by serious sin, then the path of penance through the Sacrament of Reconciliation becomes necessary for full participation in the Eucharistic Sacrifice" (37).

Therefore, in every diocese and community, particular care must be given to celebrating the Mass in a way that accords with its full liturgical import (signs, symbols, and gestures), so that the People of God may offer their conscious, active, and fruitful participation. Efforts should be made in this Holy Year to involve the entire People of God in the liturgical celebrations: children, young people, adults, elderly, disabled, prisoners, and everyone in a way that each feels seriously and peacefully involved in the mercy of God manifested in the Eucharistic celebration. The general calendar of the Jubilee foresees in each and every diocese various initiatives and celebrations that encourage the prayerful participation of every cross section of the one People of God.

It is important that special care be given to those living on the peripheries of our parishes, especially those who have distanced themselves from the Church or who have been marginalized for various reasons. Special efforts should be made so that they too receive the message that God is the Father of all who waits for everyone so that no one may be excluded from the Father's "indulgence" (*Misericordiae Vultus*, 22) or fail to receive his reconciling embrace and be restored fully to the inheritance that awaits the children of God.

The Act of Penance

Of similar importance is the Act of Penance that takes place during the introductory rites of Mass, the three forms of which should receive full use with due regard for the liturgical season. At this moment, the assembly is called to beg God's mercy, each for his or her own sins. It should be performed without haste and in due silence, giving the faithful sufficient time to recognize their sinful condition and the firm assurance of God's infinite mercy. The Act of Penance concludes with the priest pronouncing the absolution. The People of God should be reminded that this rite does not have the same force as that of the Sacrament of Penance (see *General Instruction of the Roman Missal* [*GIRM*], 51), but rather prepares us to receive the latter.

On Sundays, especially during the Easter season, the Roman Missal provides the option of substituting the penitential rite with the blessing and sprinkling of holy water in commemoration of our baptism. This gesture allows the People of God to commemorate their *status* of being "saved already" by the cross of Christ through the waters of baptism.

When the *Kyrie eleison* is sung as part of the Penitential Act, each of the acclamations is preceded by a "trope" (see *GIRM*, 52). The various options for these tropes are categorized according to the liturgical season and therefore should be chosen based on that criterion.

The Prayers of the Faithful

The prayers of the faithful should include specific intentions invoking God's mercy, as well as prayers for priests who are the primary dispensers of God's gift of mercy. The prayers of the faithful must be formulated on the basis of the true and authentic needs of the Church and the entire world, but also on those of the local community. For this reason, the generic, prefabricated prayers appearing in worship aides and liturgical publications should be used only as guidelines for crafting prayers specific to the living community so that they are "true prayers" invoking God's mercy.

The Eucharistic Prayers for Reconciliation

During this Holy Year, in accord with the principles and directives regarding the seasons and feasts of the liturgical year, it is commendable to place higher value on the Eucharistic Prayers for Reconciliation I ("Reconciliation: the return to the Father") and II ("Reconciliation with God: the Foundation of Human Harmony"). In fact, these Eucharistic prayers, especially in their prefaces and in the development of the entire anaphora, make clear the mystery of the Eucharist as the sacrifice of reconciliation and the supreme testimony of the Father's mercy, a sign of his eternal covenant to be lived out in marvel and joy that man has rediscovered salvation.

The Collection of Masses of the Blessed Virgin Mary

According to a long tradition attested to by widespread popular piety, the Church attaches such importance to the Blessed Virgin Mary on Saturday that it is often liturgically observed as a "memorial" in her honor. It is therefore opportune to highlight a few aspects of the memorial of the Blessed Virgin Mary on Saturday so that it accords more harmoniously with contemporary spirituality.

In the first place, it is important to "remember" the Blessed Virgin's attitude as a mother and a disciple "on the great Sabbath" when Christ lay in the tomb. Mary showed a singular strength of faith and hope on that day, as she was the only disciple to keep patient vigil, awaiting the Lord's resurrection. Furthermore, Saturday is a "prelude," or an "introduction," to the celebration of the Lord's Day on Sunday, the primordial feast day and weekly memorial of Christ's resurrection. Finally, the memorial of the Blessed Virgin Mary on Saturday is a "sign" that, week after week, Mary is continually present and active in the life of the Church.

The Roman Missal contains various forms for the celebration of Mass in honor of the Blessed Virgin Mary on Saturday mornings throughout the year (*per annum*) when an optional memorial in her honor is permitted. Directives can be found in the *Collection of Masses of the Blessed Virgin Mary* (*CMBMV*, 42), and specifically in the *Praenotanda* (34-36). Similarly, the Liturgy of the Hours also includes an optional Office for the Blessed Virgin Mary on Saturday on Saturdays *per annum*.

Whenever permitted by the liturgical calendar and on memorials of Our Lady lacking proper prayers, the Mass settings in the *Collection of Masses of the Blessed Virgin Mary* may be used, especially those that particularly extol the figure of Mary as the primary witness of the Father's love and mercy: "For he has regarded the low estate of his handmaiden ... all generations will call me blessed" (Lk 1:48-49).

Thus the following Mass settings would be appropriate during the Jubilee Year: *The Blessed Virgin Mary, Help of Christians*, where in the prayer after Communion it is asked of the Father, through the intercession of the Blessed Virgin Mary, to help us cast aside "the old ways of sin and put on Jesus Christ, the author of the new creation" (*CMBMV*, 42); *The Blessed Virgin Mary, Cause of Our Joy*, where sharing in the joy of Mary, the Father's beloved daughter, we are called to rejoice in our merciful encounter with the good Father (see *CMBMV*, 34); *The Blessed Virgin Mary at the Foot of the Cross*, where we ask that the whole "human race, deceived by the wiles of the devil, might become a new and resplendent creation." We continue to pray, "Grant that your people may put aside their inheritance of sin and put on the newness of life won by Christ the Redeemer" (*CMBMV*, 11-12); *Holy Mary, the New Eve*, where we ask that "we may reject the old ways of sin" and "embrace wholeheartedly the new commandment of love" (*CMBMV*, 20); *The Virgin Mary, Fountain of Salvation*, who brought forth God's "eternal Word, Jesus Christ, the fountain of living water" (*CMBMV*, 31); *Holy Mary, Queen and Mother of Mercy*, "always attentive to the voice of her children, seeking to win your compassion for them, and asking your forgiveness for their sins" (*CMBMV*, 39); *The Blessed Virgin Mary, Mother of Reconciliation*, who, chosen by God at the foot of the Cross to be "the Mother of reconciliation for sinners," we pray may intercede for us to "obtain pardon for our sins" and a renewed sense of the Father's love (*CMBMV*, 14); and *The Blessed Virgin Mary, Mother and Mediatrix of Grace*, with whom we ask God to transform our humble offering into the sacrament of redemption, "so that what Christ our Mediator has established as the means of our reconciliation with you may become for us the source of grace and the enduring fountain of eternal salvation" (*CMBMV*, 30).

Masses and Prayers for Various Needs and Votive Masses

Among the Mass settings and prayers "for various needs" and the options for votive Masses, some make explicit reference to the mercy of God that has always been, and always will be, available to those who honor him (see Ps 103:17). Among these settings, special attention should be given to the Masses *for Reconciliation, for the Forgiveness of Sins, for Peace,* as well as *the Mystery of the Cross, the Most Precious Blood of Our Lord Jesus Christ, the Most Sacred Heart of Jesus,* and *the Mercy of God.*

CHAPTER THREE

Praying as One

In order to celebrate the Lord's mercy, we must also pay attention to the prayers that accompany the Christian life of many faithful and constitute a major part of the Church's liturgy. These also will be important means of experiencing God's mercy and helping us live that mercy as fully as possible.

The Liturgy of Hours

The communal recitation of the Liturgy of Hours will make a positive contribution to the Holy Year, especially when it comes to the two hinges: morning prayer and evening prayer.

The Church beautifully begins her daily prayer with these words: "O God, come to my assistance. O Lord, make haste to help me" (Ps 70:2). The help we beg of God is already an extension of his mercy toward us. He comes to save us from the condition of weakness in which we live. Day after day, touched by his compassion, we in turn become more compassionate toward those we encounter along the way. "In a special way the Psalms bring to the fore the grandeur of his merciful action: 'He forgives all your iniquity, he heals all your diseases, he redeems your life from the pit, he crowns you with steadfast love and mercy' (Ps 103:3-4). Another psalm, in an even more explicit way, attests to the concrete signs of his mercy:

'He executes justice for the oppressed; he gives food to the hungry. The Lord sets the prisoners free; the Lord opens the eyes of the blind. The Lord lifts up those who are bowed down … but the way of the wicked he brings to ruin' (Ps 146:7-9)" (*Misericordiae Vultus*, 6). Moreover, the Psalms communicate in an outstanding way the thoughts and feelings of a praying heart: thanksgiving, penance, a plea for mercy, praise, and glorification.

When the liturgy allows for it, and especially when the faithful are gathered for prayer, care must be taken to choose psalms that clearly emphasize reconciliation and mercy. Some of these are mentioned by Pope Francis in *Misericordiae Vultus*, specifically, Psalms 25, 50, 103, 146-147, and 136.

Other psalms are suggested in *The Psalms of Mercy*, by the Pontifical Council for Promotion of the New Evangelization, which also contains accompanying biblical reflections inspired by the Psalms themselves. These would be useful for effective catechesis and for helping the People of God appreciate the beauty and richness of these poems of praise.

It would also be desirable for the psalms to be sung. In this way, the music makes clear the "melody" of the Father's mercy in harmony with the love of the Trinity. This particularly holds true for the Magnificat, the Virgin's canticle, which shines out as a hymn of praise to the mercy of the Almighty: "He has looked upon his lowly handmaid … his mercy reaches from age to age for those who fear him.… He has come to the help of Israel his servant, mindful of his mercy" (see Lk 1:46-55, Jerusalem Bible).

Eucharistic Adoration

The Holy Year also provides an opportunity to deepen our appreciation for the value of Eucharistic Adoration in individual communities, during which we pray for mercy and peace before Our Lord present in the Sacrament. This prayer, with due respect for the silence proper to it, can be accompanied by occasional scriptural readings that speak of the Lord's mercy, or excerpts from commentaries by the Church Fathers. While the Blessed Sacrament is exposed, prayers, songs, and readings should be chosen and executed in such a way that the faithful continuously direct their devotion toward Christ the Lord.

Ecumenical and Interreligious Prayer

In *Misericordiae Vultus*, the pope recommends that particular attention be paid to the ecumenical and interreligious nature of the Jubilee Year so that significant steps can be made toward mitigating, and one day to eliminating completely, every prejudice toward our sister churches and other religious confessions in the search for unity, mutual respect, and peace in the hearts of all peoples: "There is an aspect of mercy that goes beyond the confines of the Church. It relates us to Judaism and Islam, both of which consider mercy to be one of God's most important attributes.... I trust that this Jubilee year celebrating the mercy of God will foster an encounter with these religions and with other noble religious traditions; may it open us to even more fervent dialogue so that we might know and understand one another better; may it eliminate every form of closed-mindedness and disrespect, and drive out every form of violence and discrimination" (23).

Therefore, fifty years after the promulgation of *Nostra Aetate* (Declaration on the Relationshiop of the Church to Non-Christian Religions) at the Second Vatican Council, we are called to deepen our awareness of the necessity to pray for the gift of unity among Christians and for peace and brotherhood among all religions. This prayer is succinctly expressed in the universal prayers offered in the liturgy of Good Friday and is perpetuated in our communities throughout the year, especially during the Week of Prayer for Christian Unity. For this reason, it is opportune for every Christian community to set aside times of prayer to implore God for these gifts. It is also good, especially at cathedral churches, to organize celebrations of the Word with brother Christians of other confessions and moments of mutual exchange and dialogue with members of other religions. It is important for bishops to promote these opportunities within their own dioceses, involving others with the skills to organize such events, so that they may be effective opportunities to show a shared respect and joy of living together and of interceding for one another, imploring the mercy of the Almighty.

To make this prayer an even more intense and vigorous plea for God's gift of unity, which will reach its zenith in a common sharing of the Eucharist at a single table, use can be made, whenever the liturgical season permits, of the prayers found in the Mass for Christian Unity and the Mass setting for *Holy Mary, Mother of Unity* (*CMBMV*, 38).

Popular Piety

In his apostolic exhortation *Evangelii Nuntiandi*, Blessed Paul VI had this to say about popular religiosity and piety: "It manifests a thirst for God which only the simple and poor can know. It makes people capable of generosity and sacrifice even to the point of heroism, when it is a question of manifesting belief. It involves an acute awareness of profound attributes of God: fatherhood, providence, loving and constant presence. It engenders interior attitudes rarely observed to the same degree elsewhere: patience, the sense of the cross in daily life, detachment, openness to others, devotion" (48). The richness of popular piety was underscored once again by Pope Francis in *Evangelii Gaudium*. It would be useful during the Holy Year to make use of the *Directory on Popular Piety and the Liturgy*, which is a wonderful resource for various forms of popular religiosity in accord with the liturgical year.

Pilgrimage

The practice of pilgrimage takes on special significance in the Holy Year insofar as it represents the journey each of us must make in this life. Even to reach the Holy Door in Rome or the Door of Mercy in any particular diocese, everyone, according to his or her abilities, will have to make a "pilgrimage." "This will be a sign that mercy is also a goal to reach and requires dedication and sacrifice. May pilgrimage be an impetus to conversion: by crossing the threshold of the Holy Door, we will find the strength to embrace God's mercy and dedicate ourselves to being merciful with others as the Father has been with us" (*Misericordiae Vultus*, 14).

Thus in every diocese it is commendable to designate some destinations for pilgrimages, such as the cathedral church, a shrine, or other places particularly meaningful to the people's sense of Christian piety and where the bishop has decreed that a Door of Mercy be opened. Pilgrims are encouraged to make at least a part of this journey by foot to signify the sacrifice and commitment needed to convert and taste with greater enthusiasm the joy of reaching the ultimate goal, Christ our Lord. The pilgrimage can be accompanied by meditations on the Word of God or by chanting the *Psalms of Mercy* collected in the booklet entitled *The Psalms of Mercy*. It is well-known that pilgrimage is one of the most preferred means of approaching and preparing ourselves to receive the Sacrament of Reconciliation. Thus priests should encourage the People of God to approach the gift of the Father's mercy in this sacrament. At the same time, may there not be a lack of confessors willing to make the time to receive penitents, fully conscious of their call to absolve sins and to make themselves instruments of God's mercy of which they have been made dispensers.

Indulgences are another inherent aspect of the Jubilee. It is important to remind the People of God that, given they have the required dispositions, they can experience the holiness of the Church which participates in all of the benefits of Christ's redemption, so that mercy can reach even into the farthest extremes already touched by God's love.

Veneration of the Crucified Christ
During the Paschal Triduum, Good Friday is the day most especially dedicated to the Lord's passion, and it is therefore the

day par excellence when "Adoration of the Holy Cross" takes place. However, insofar as the cross is a true icon of the Father's mercy, this gesture is also deeply embedded in popular piety. Hence it is also a special point of reference in this Holy Year. In fact, along the entire arc of the Lenten season, Friday, according to the Church's ancient tradition, is the day when we commemorate Christ's passion, and the faithful therefore willingly direct their piety toward the mystery of the Cross. By contemplating the crucified Savior, the faithful grasp the meaning of the immense and unjust suffering of Jesus, holy and innocent, who suffered for the salvation of mankind, and they comprehend the value of his abiding love and the efficacy of his redeeming sacrifice.

The many expressions of devotion to the Crucified Christ take on particular significance in churches dedicated to the mystery of the Cross, in which relics of the *lignum Crucis* are often reserved. During this Holy Year, therefore, and in accord with the liturgical seasons, consideration should be given to special celebrations in which scriptural passages are read that deal with Our Lord's passion. There should also be songs and prayers related to the Passion, as well as times for exposing, processing with, and blessing the faithful with the cross. These events can be organized by the numerous confraternities throughout the world that originally were born to stir up the souls of the faithful with celebrations involving the cross, especially in those places where famous relics of the *lignum Crucis* are kept. "Devotion to the Cross, however, sometimes requires a certain enlightenment. The faithful should be taught to place the Cross in its essential reference to the Resurrection of Christ: the Cross, the empty tomb, the Death and Resurrection of Christ are indispensable in the Gospel narrative of God's salvific plan. In the Christian faith, the Cross is an expression of the triumph of Christ over the powers of darkness. Hence, it is adorned with precious stones and is a sign of blessing when made upon one's self, or on others or on objects" (*Directory on Popular Piety and the Liturgy*, 128). For this reason, especially during the Easter season, the cross can be adorned or decorated with flowers representing Christ's victory over death by the Cross. The mixed fragrance of death and resurrection, of the one and indivisible Paschal Mystery, should also characterize all those devotions that highlight one particular aspect of Christ's passion and are widely spread among the People of God, such as the *"Ecce Homo,"* "Christ scorned," and "Christ wearing the crown of thorns and the purple cloak" (see Jn 19:5) whom Pilate shows to the crowds; also "the holy wounds of Christ," especially his pierced side and the life-giving blood that flows from it (Jn 19:34), the instruments of his passion such as the pillar at which he was scourged, the steps of the praetorium, the crown of thorns, the nails, the spear that pierced his side, and the holy shroud or burial cloth.

The Way of the Cross

The Jubilee Year is an opportune time to choose carefully the biblical readings, reflections, and gestures that accompany the Way of the Cross as a popular expression of the Father's love manifested in the sacrifice of his Son for all humanity. Indeed, a number of aspects of Christian spirituality converge in the pious practice of the *Via Crucis:* the idea that life is a journey or a pilgrimage; that the mystery of the Cross is a bridge that crosses over from the exile of this earthly life to the heavenly homeland; the desire to conform oneself completely to Christ's passion; the requirements of the *sequela Christi,* according to which a disciple must take up his cross daily and walk behind the Master (see Lk 9:23).

Devotion to the Blessed Virgin Mary

Our thoughts will turn in a special way to the Mother of Mercy in this Holy Year. The sweetness of her gaze will accompany us so that we may all rediscover the joy of God's tenderness. Pope Francis, in addition to the other Marian feast days of the liturgical year, wished to place special emphasis on Saturday and Sunday, October 8 and 9, dates near the memorial of the Blessed Virgin Mary of the

Rosary: "No one has penetrated the profound mystery of the incarnation like Mary. Her entire life was patterned after the presence of mercy made flesh. The Mother of the Crucified and Risen One has entered the sanctuary of divine mercy because she participated intimately in the mystery of his love" (*Misericordiae Vultus*, 24).

The Rosary of the Blessed Virgin Mary

Tradition and popular piety teach us that the prayer of the rosary is the simplest and most direct way to invoke God's mercy through the intercession of the Virgin Mary. The recitation of the Rosary is often accompanied by passages from Scripture, the works of the Church Fathers, or other spiritual authors. In this Holy Year, it would be good to choose passages that particularly highlight the motherly face of the one who first experienced the Father's mercy, who, in turn, looked upon the lowliness of his servant (see Lk 1:48). "Let us address her in the words of the *Salve Regina*, a prayer ever ancient and ever new, so that she may never tire of turning her merciful eyes upon us, and make us worthy to contemplate the face of mercy, her Son Jesus" (*Misericordiae Vultus*, 24).

Recourse to the intercession of the saints will also be important in this Holy Year, especially through the recitation of litanies. Especially during pilgrimages, "the Church lives within the communion of the saints. In the Eucharist, this communion, which is a gift from God, becomes a spiritual union binding us to the saints and blessed ones whose number is beyond counting (cf. Rv 7:4). Their holiness comes to the aid of our weakness in a way that enables the Church, with her maternal prayers and her way of life, to fortify the weakness of some with the strength of others" (*Misericordiae Vultus*, 22).

The Litany of Divine Mercy should also be held in high esteem throughout this Jubilee Year.

Veneration of the Blessed Virgin Mary, Our Lady of Sorrows

Because of its doctrinal and pastoral significance, it will be important to cultivate a devotion to the sorrows of the Blessed

Virgin Mary, especially on the liturgical memorial of Our Lady of Sorrows on September 15. Joined most intimately to the passion of her Son and close to him when he was raised on the cross (see Jn 19:25-27), Mary, in her Immaculate Conception, is the first to enjoy the fruits of the redemption and mercy of the Almighty flowing from the sacrifice of Christ on the cross, and is the primary witness of divine mercy, who intercedes with us in the presence of her Son that we may obtain mercy. For this reason, the third edition of the *Roman Missal* suggests that the hymn *Stabat Mater* accompany the Veneration of the Cross on Good Friday. This hymn can also be used on other occasions as well, especially during the *Via Crucis*, and it would be opportune to explain its profound meaning as an expression of faith to the People of God through catechesis.

Besides processions with an image Our Lady of Sorrows, a practice particularly widespread during Lent and on Good Friday, there are other manifestations of popular piety that may be promoted in this Jubilee Year: the *Planctus Mariae*, an acute expression of pain, as well as other literary and musical works in which the Virgin weeps not only over the death of her son but over the waywardness of his people and the sinfulness of humanity; the *Ora della Desolata*, called *El pésame* in some regions of Latin America, in which the faithful, by means of emotional expressions of devotion, "keep company" with the Mother of our Savior as she is immersed in deep pain, focusing the pain of the whole universe on the death of her Son. These pious practices should not be limited to mere human feeling in the presence of a mother deprived of her son, but rather should be carried out with ardent faith in the Resurrection. They must help us to comprehend the grandeur of Christ's redemptive love and his mother's participation in it, to learn from her how to keep vigil at the countless crosses carried by the men and women of our time.

Chaplet of Divine Mercy
In recent times, in light of the messages that St. Faustina Kowalska received from Our Lord, the Octave of Easter has been a

time of particular devotion to the divine mercy poured out from Christ through his death and resurrection, the font of the Spirit who forgives sin and restores joy to those who have been saved. This devotion has given rise to the *Chaplet of Divine Mercy*, a devotion practiced by many faithful that, especially in this Jubilee Year, can be promoted and encouraged among the People of God. When *Divine Mercy Sunday* is celebrated on April 3, 2016, Pope Francis will receive all those who, through various forms of consecrated life and pious associations of the faithful, make divine mercy their program of life.

This Jubilee Year thus invites us to join Pope Francis and these communities in turning our gaze and prayer to God. As Pope Francis writes in *Misericordiae Vultus*, "Our prayer also extends to the saints and blessed ones who made divine mercy their mission in life. I think especially of the great apostle of mercy, St. Faustina Kowalska. May she, who was called to enter the depths of divine mercy, intercede for us and obtain for us the grace of living and walking always according to the mercy of God and with an unwavering trust in his love" (24).

In any case, "since the liturgy of the Second Sunday of Easter or Divine Mercy Sunday — as it is now called — is the natural locus in which, to express man's acceptance of the Redeemer's mercy, the faithful should be taught to understand this devotion in the light of the liturgical celebrations of these Easter days. Indeed, the paschal Christ is the definitive incarnation of mercy, his living sign which is both historico-salvific and eschatological. At the same time, the Easter liturgy places the words of the psalm on our lips: 'shall sing forever of the Lord's mercy' (Ps 89:2)" (*Directory on Popular Piety and the Liturgy*, 154).

Prayer for the Jubilee of Mercy

It is worth recalling that the Holy Father wished that a special prayer be composed for the Holy Year. This *Prayer for the Jubilee of Mercy* can be recited in groups or individually. It will be a sign of unity among all communities as they implore the Lord's mercy so that this ecclesial event can bear the fruit of conversion and an encounter with the good Father.

Special Places During the Jubilee

Certain places and things will receive special attention during the Jubilee, including the *altar*, the *door*, the *baptismal font*, and *the place where the Sacrament of Reconciliation is celebrated (the confessional)*. As emerges throughout the Church's history, the mystogogical dimension of these places assumes special importance especially among the people for whom, more than verbal catechesis, images, and icons play a fundamental role in Christian initiation and to handing on the mysteries of the Christian faith to catechumens.

The Altar

If the altar is held in such high esteem throughout the liturgical year as the church's sacramental center point, and the place where the sacrifice of Christ is offered and the Eucharistic banquet is partaken of, it assumes even more significance in this Holy Year. In fact, the altar becomes the point of convergence not only of the Church's sacramentality, but of the Father's infinite mercy revealed in many different ways, preeminently in the sacrifice of his Son, the perfect and saving culmination of his mercy.

For this reason, even though every place associated with worship needs diligent care, the altar occupies pride of place. It therefore needs to be cared for in such a way that, in its modest decoration (flowers, altar cloth, candles, etc.), it manifests the great mystery celebrated upon it and refers to the cross, which should also be placed near it and remain in close relationship with it. The faithful should be imbued with great respect for the altar by avoiding the placement of any extraneous objects or inappropriate linens on it; it should also be kept in mind that the altar is not the place from which to preside over the assembly or proclaim the readings, both of which have their respective places — namely, the chair and the ambo. The altar is properly the place of the Liturgy of the Eucharist and the anaphora. Therefore, may it not be "permanently occupied" by the priest or other ministers during ceremonies. In fact, whenever there is physical movement from one place to another as the liturgy proceeds, this movement expresses the liturgy's mystogogical dimension in introducing the People of God to the mysteries of faith through sensible signs.

The Door

While the atrium is the space indicating the Church's maternal embrace, the door represents Christ, the "gate for the sheep" (Jn 10:7). The iconological meaning of the door should inspire its iconography, which should be neither arbitrary nor random, but rather constitutive of the very place. This is all the more true in the case of the Door of Mercy. Indeed, this door, both in its majestic appearance and in its decoration, must draw attention to that which it represents in a simple and noble way. Respect should be shown to the door, therefore, both in its iconography and its decoration, as well as in the processional movements of the liturgy and in the celebration of the sacraments, such as the *Rite of Acceptance* and the *Rite of Baptism*, in the entrance procession at Mass, and in the acceptance of the casket in the *Rite of Christian Funeral*.

The Baptismal Font

Mother Church gives birth to her children from the baptismal font, for it is there that she immerses them in the waters of Christ's paschal mystery. The font therefore should be highlighted during the Jubilee so that it stands as a constant reminder of the dignity that God the Father has raised them to. It should be a place that reminds us of the white garment of baptism in which every Christian was clothed on the day of his or her rebirth. It should also recall the "ring" of royal dignity that each Christian has been given through the action of the Holy Spirit. Let us not forget the summons to the prophet who, having been touched on the ears and mouth with the burning ember of God's mercy, is called to announce the Father's goodness and patience in the presence of the sinfulness of mankind (see Is 6:7).

The most significant objects adorning the baptismal font are undoubtedly the candle (for this reason the Paschal candle and its stand should not be lacking in those times when the liturgical calendar requires it, even if the font is not being used), together with flowers that remind us of life and rebirth. The font should be accessible and easily recognizable by the faithful even when not in use.

The Confessional

The Sacrament of Reconciliation requires a fitting and welcoming place for its celebration. Care must be taken that, while this space is connected to the main body of the church, it is favorable to the penitential act and fosters a dialogue between penitent and minister, protecting the privacy of the penitent and allowing for individual confession. It must be a welcoming atmosphere and allow for the possibility of receiving the sacrament in the traditional way. It should also include a stand upon which the Word of God can be opened, easily accessible to the penitent so that he or she can meditate on the words of Holy Scripture. In short, it should be a "place" where true conversion takes place.

In some way the connection between the confessional and the baptismal font, the fundamental anchor of salvation, should be highlighted. Indeed, if baptism is the sacrament through which every Christian is immersed in the salvation brought about by Christ's paschal mystery, then reconciliation, the second anchor of salvation, restores the sinner to the dignity of being a child of God, saved by his mercy.

Spiritual Communion

For many centuries the faithful, especially those inhibited from participating in the Eucharist for any reason, have practiced *spiritual communion* as a way of uniting themselves to the Lord in their daily lives; the practice of spiritual communion is encouraged by many saints. St. Teresa of Ávila, for example, writes to her followers: "My daughters, when you listen to Holy Mass without approaching to receive communion, be sure to receive communion spiritually and remain in a state of recollection. This practice has many benefits, and by means of it you will burn with greater love for God" (*The Way of Perfection*, 35, 1).

St. Alphonsus Liguori exhorts the faithful to practice spiritual communion several times a day, especially whenever visiting the Most Blessed Sacrament. He says that there are two things necessary to make this communion: the first is the ardent desire to receive Jesus sacramentally, and the second is a loving embrace, as if he were already received. St. John Bosco reminds us, "If you are unable to receive holy Communion sacramentally, at least make a spiritual communion, which consists in an ardent desire to receive Jesus in your heart" (see G. B. Lemoyne, *Memorie Biografiche del Venerabile Don Giovanni Bosco*, Vol. III, p. 13). The Congregation for the Doctrine of the Faith, in a letter in 1983, also commended this practice to remain close to the Lord in daily life: "Individual faithful or communities who because of persecution or lack of priests are deprived of the holy Eucharist for either a short or longer period of time, do not thereby lack the grace of the Redeemer. If they are intimately animated by a desire for the sacrament and united in prayer with the whole Church, and call upon the Lord and raise their hearts to him, by virtue of the Holy Spirit they live in communion with the whole Church, the living body of Christ, and with the Lord himself. Through their desire for the sacrament in union with the Church, no matter how distant they may be physically, they are intimately and really united to her and therefore receive the fruits of the sacrament; whereas those who would wrongly attempt to take upon themselves the right to confect the Eucharistic Mystery end up by having their community closed in on itself" (*Sacerdotium Ministeriale*, III, 4).

CHAPTER FOUR

Lectio Divina

1. Merciful just like the Father

The Word of God
... is heard

Then [Jesus] said, "A man had two sons, and the younger son said to his father, 'Father, give me the share of your estate that should come to me.' So the father divided the property between them. After a few days, the younger son collected all his belongings and set off to a distant country where he squandered his inheritance on a life of dissipation. When he had freely spent everything, a severe famine struck that country, and he found himself in dire need. So he hired himself out to one of the local citizens who sent him to his farm to tend the swine. And he longed to eat his fill of the pods on which the swine fed, but nobody gave him any. Coming to his senses he thought, 'How many of my father's hired workers have more than enough food to eat, but here am I, dying from hunger. I shall get up and go to my father and I shall say to him, "Father, I have sinned against heaven and against you. I no longer deserve to be called your son; treat me as you would treat one of your hired workers.'" So he got up and went back to his father. While he was still a long way off, his father caught sight of him, and was filled with compassion. He ran to his son, embraced him and kissed him. His son said to him, 'Father, I have sinned against heaven and against you; I no longer deserve to be called your son.' But his father ordered his servants, 'Quickly bring the finest robe and put it on him; put a ring on his finger and sandals on his feet. Take the fattened calf and slaughter it. Then let us celebrate with a feast, because this son of mine was dead, and has come to life again; he was lost, and has been found.' Then the celebration began. Now the older son had been out in the field and, on his way back, as he neared the house, he heard the sound of music and dancing. He called one of the servants and asked what this might mean. The servant said to him, 'Your brother has returned and your father has slaughtered the fattened calf because he has him back safe and sound.' He became angry, and when he refused to enter the house, his father came out and pleaded with him. He said to his father in reply, 'Look, all these years I served you and not once did I disobey your orders; yet you never gave me even a young goat to feast on with my friends. But when your son returns who swallowed up your property with prostitutes, for him you slaughter the fattened calf.' He said to him, 'My son, you are here with me always; everything I have is yours. But now we must celebrate and rejoice, because your brother was dead and has come to life again; he was lost and has been found.'" (Luke 15:11-32)

… and meditated

At the time this parable was told, the Jewish law proscribed that the firstborn son received two-thirds of his father's inheritance, while the younger son received a third. Without hesitation, the father gives his younger son the part due to him. While the younger son squanders the inheritance through a dissolute life in a far away land, the other two-thirds are kept safe and managed by the older son. According to the normal way of thinking about what is just and fair, if and when the younger son returns home, he won't expect to receive anything from his father or older brother. The serious sin of the younger son can, at the most, be forgiven, but not forgotten! Should the father forget this, his older son will be there to remind him. This is what the law of retribution would have demanded: a good recompense for whoever has done good, and a bad one for whoever has done evil.

In reality, the parable flies in the face of the law of inheritance and thus reveals the excessive love of the father. The father does not summon the two sons before him, he does not verify whether the younger son has really repented, he does not ask what happened to his inheritance; rather, he organizes a feast with a lot of music and dancing. The father's treatment of the older son is also inconceivable: he doesn't summon him when he returns from the fields, where he has been working for his family all day, nor does he seek his opinion about how he should treat the younger son. The parable that most reveals God's human face portrays it *too* well and without defect: God does not lack humanity, he is *too* human!

Unlike the father who transgresses the law about how to divide his estate, the two brothers are unable to go beyond the logic of giving in order to receive.

In distinction from the father who transgresses the law regarding the distribution of his inheritance, the two brothers are not able to go beyond the logic of giving in order to receive. The younger son receives the part of the inheritance that falls to him, squanders it on prostitutes, and decides to return home when nothing is left. In this condition, the most he can hope for is that he will be readmitted to his father's estate as a wage laborer; it's not so much repentance that drives him, but utter starvation!

The older son is also involved when it comes to "just" retribution: he has served his father faithfully for years, he has never disobeyed one of his commandments, and he expected to receive at least a kid goat to celebrate with his friends. When faced with the compassion of his father, the elder son accuses him of haven broken the law of just distribution; he's not even able to consider the son of his own father his brother. Rather, he refers to him as "this son of yours." By fitting his father into the neat box of "distributor of the inheritance" he fails to recognize him as a bother and his brother as a brother.

(Adapted from *The Parables of Mercy*)

... and prayed

Psalm 51:3-6,10-15

Have mercy on me, God, in accord with your merciful love;
    in your abundant compassion blot out my transgressions.
Thoroughly wash away my guilt;
    and from my sin cleanse me.
For I know my transgressions;
    my sin is always before me.
Against you, you alone have I sinned;
    I have done what is evil in your eyes
So that you are just in your word,
    and without reproach in your judgment
You will let me hear gladness and joy;
    the bones you have crushed will rejoice.

Turn away your face from my sins;
    blot out all my iniquities.
A clean heart create for me, God;
    renew within me a steadfast spirit.
Do not drive me from before your face,
    nor take from me your holy spirit.

Restore to me the gladness of your salvation;
  uphold me with a willing spirit.
I will teach the wicked your ways,
  that sinners may return to you.

Psalm 25:4-7

Make known to me your ways, LORD;
  teach me your paths.
Guide me by your fidelity and teach me,
  for you are God my savior,
    for you I wait all the day long.
Remember your compassion and your mercy, O LORD,
  for they are ages old.
Remember no more the sins of my youth;
  remember me according to your mercy,
  because of your goodness, LORD.

2. Who is my neighbor?

The Word of God

... is heard

There was a scholar of the law who stood up to test him and said, "Teacher, what must I do to inherit eternal life?" Jesus said to him, "What is written in the law? How do you read it?" He said in reply, "You shall love the Lord, your God, with all your heart, with all your being, with all your strength, and with all your mind, and your neighbor as yourself." He replied to him, "You have answered correctly; do this and you will live."

But because he wished to justify himself, he said to Jesus, "And who is my neighbor?" Jesus replied, "A man fell victim to robbers as he went down from Jerusalem to Jericho. They stripped and beat him and went off leaving him half-dead. A priest happened to be going down that road, but when he saw him, he passed by on the opposite side. Likewise a Levite came to the place, and when he saw him, he passed by on the opposite side. But a Samaritan traveler who came upon him was moved with compassion at the sight. He approached the victim, poured oil and wine over his wounds and bandaged them. Then he lifted him up on his own animal, took him to an inn and cared for him. The next day he took out two silver coins and gave them to the innkeeper with the instruction, 'Take care of him. If you spend more than what I have given you, I shall repay you on my way back.' Which of these three, in your opinion, was neighbor to the robbers' victim?" He answered, "The one who treated him with mercy." Jesus said to him, "Go and do likewise." (Luke 10:25-37)

... and meditated

As usual, the characters in this parable are anonymous so that Jesus can concentrate on their religious and ethnic identities. Jesus begins in a far-off place: he has not yet reached Jericho on his journey to Jerusalem, but he is already thinking of a man who comes down from the Holy City toward Jericho. The road connecting these two cities, which were about 17 miles apart, was dangerous because it crossed Wadi Quelt. While Jerusalem was 2,460 feet above sea level, Jericho was about 1,300 feet below sea level. For this reason, as the parable suggests, it was necessary to "come down" from Jerusalem to reach Jericho. Jesus says that some robbers attacked the man and left him half-dead. The condition of the robbed man is the hinge upon which the entire parable turns. Is it possible for someone to come into contact with a half-dead man and not become contaminated?

It is no accident that the three characters who come across the victim are all important to the question of how the one God is to be worshiped: a priest who goes up and comes down from Jerusalem to perform his priestly service at the Temple; a Levite who belongs to the priestly class, but who can also be exempt from priestly service; and a Samaritan. Precisely here the expectations of the listeners are completely overturned, for the normal triad is usually composed of a priest, a Levite, and an Israelite (see Dt 18:1; 27:9). Making the Samaritan the third figure is quite provocative for, according to the Jewish mindset, he is to be considered impure insofar as he is a foreigner.

According to the Mosaic Law, whoever touches a corpse remains unclean for a week. If he performs a cultic act while contaminated, he is to be expelled from Israel (see Nm 19:11-13). This rule holds all the more firmly for a priest, even if he has touched a deceased relative (Lv 21:1-4). The parable thus places these two figures in a tough situation where they have to choose between observing the rules regarding cultic purity and helping a half-dead man. In any case, we have to keep in mind that the cultural norms do not excuse the priest and the Levite, because in situations like that given in the parable they are obliged to help the dying man; both, however, see him and pass by.

The parable reaches a turning point when it is specified that the Samaritan "had compassion" on the dying man (v. 33); so much so that at the end of the parable the doctor of the Law acknowledges that the neighbor is the one how "showed mercy to him" (v. 37). It is worth pausing for a moment to examine more closely the word expressing the Samaritan's compassion. The Greek verb *splanch-nízomai* ("to have compassion," or "to suffer with") is derived from the noun *splánchna* which refers to the human inner organs, including the heart. The common way of thinking at the time of Jesus was that the inner organs expressed one's sentiments: love, compassion, and mercy. The Samaritan does not allow himself simply to look at the dying man on the road, he feels bound up with his suffering in his innermost being; and it is this visceral compassion that puts into motion everything the Samaritan does to save the dying man.

True compassion is not just a feeling but an action that leads to true care for the other. In the specific details of this parable, Jesus recounts the help this Samaritan gives to the dying man: he approaches him, cleanses and bandages his wounds, sets him on his donkey, takes him to an inn, and cares for him there. Once the robbed man survives the first night, which is the riskiest, the Samaritan notices that he is still alive and gives the innkeeper two denarii, which equaled the wages of two days labor. As he is leaving to continue his journey, he guarantees the innkeeper that if there are other expenses, he will pay for them on the way back.

Throughout the entire parable, nothing is said about the dying man: neither his origins nor his social status are mentioned. All the attention is placed on the one caring for him, the one who gives his very self for the man's well-being. True compassion involves making sacrifices for the good of the other person, no matter how much time and money it costs. According to St. Ambrose of Milan: "Mercy, not kinship, makes someone a neighbor" (*Exposition on the Gospel of Luke*, 7, 84).

(Adapted from *The Parables of Mercy*)

... and prayed

Psalm 41:2-4

Blessed the one concerned for the poor;
>   on a day of misfortune, the Lord delivers him.
The Lord keeps and preserves him,
>   makes him blessed in the land,
>   and does not betray him to his enemies.
The Lord sustains him on his sickbed,
>   you turn down his bedding whenever he is ill.

Psalm 142:2-4,6-8

With my own voice I cry to the Lord;
>   with my own voice I beseech the Lord.
Before him I pour out my complaint,
>   tell of my distress in front of him.
When my spirit is faint within me,
>   you know my path.
As I go along this path,
>   they have hidden a trap for me.
I cry out to you, Lord,
>   I say, You are my refuge,
>   my portion in the land of the living.
Listen to my cry for help,
>   for I am brought very low.
Rescue me from my pursuers,
>   for they are too strong for me.
Lead my soul from prison,
>   that I may give thanks to your name.
Then the righteous shall gather around me
>   because you have been good to me.

3. His many sins are forgiven him, because he has loved much

The Word of God

... is heard

A Pharisee invited him to dine with him, and he entered the Pharisee's house and reclined at table. Now there was a sinful woman in the city who learned that he was at table in the house of the Pharisee. Bringing an alabaster flask of ointment, she stood behind him at his feet weeping and began to bathe his feet with her tears. Then she wiped them with her hair, kissed them, and anointed them with the ointment. When the Pharisee who had invited him saw this he said to himself, "If this man were a prophet, he would know who and what sort of woman this is who is touching him, that she is a sinner." Jesus said to him in reply, "Simon, I have something to say to you." "Tell me, teacher," he said. "Two people were in debt to a certain creditor; one owed five hundred days' wages and the other owed fifty. Since they were unable to repay the debt, he forgave it for both. Which of them will love him more?" Simon said in reply, "The one, I suppose, whose larger debt was forgiven." He said to him, "You have judged rightly." Then he turned to the woman and said to Simon, "Do you see this woman? When I entered your house, you did not give me water for my feet, but she has bathed them with her tears and wiped them with her hair. You did not give me a kiss, but she has not ceased kissing my feet since the time I entered. You did not anoint my head with oil, but she anointed my feet with ointment. So I tell you, her many sins have been forgiven; hence, she has shown great love. But the one to whom little is forgiven, loves little." He said to her, "Your sins are forgiven." The others at table

said to themselves, "Who is this who even forgives sins?"
But he said to the woman, "Your faith has saved you; go
in peace." (Luke 7:36-50)

... and meditated

Jesus' compassion for sinners is full of humanity and gratu-
itousness; he has nothing in mind but the sinner's good. This brief
parable clarifies what is going on in Simon's house with the sinful
woman. For as short as it is, the parable is replete with meaning. In
order not to reveal right away how the parable relates to the present
situation, Jesus tells the story of two debtors and one creditor. As
usual, Jesus does not name the debtors and creditors explicitly so
that he can draw attention to the story's central message. The first
borrower owes five hundred denarii to the creditor and the second
fifty. The disproportion by a factor of ten is significant. To get a
better idea of the value of the two amounts, fifty denarii correspond
to approximately two months of wages, and five hundred denarii
correspond to about two and a half years of hired labor.

Jesus makes it clear that the two debtors are unable to pay back
the owed amounts and are completely at the mercy of their creditor.
In this parable, the characters don't say a word. We are not privy to
any dialogue between the debtors and the creditor. All the attention
is focused on the verb "they were forgiven," expressing the grace
each receives from the creditor. It is this completely gratuitous favor
that leads Jesus to ask Simon, "Which of them will love him more?"

Simon, still not realizing Jesus is testing him, answers that the
debtor to whom the larger amount was forgiven will love the creditor more. Simon's own response unmasks him and incriminates
him! If he had been more attentive to the parable, he would have
understood that, insofar as any sin is an incurred debt, grace alone
can forgive the debt anyone has to God. Clearly, Simon has yet to
get over the shock of seeing the sinful woman receive such forgiving
grace from Jesus.

The parable shows what is really happening in the house of the

Pharisee. Simon is akin to the debtor who owes his master only two months labor, and for this reason he offers no water for Jesus to wash his feet; he gives him no kiss, nor does he anoint his head with oil. The sinful woman is like the debtor who owes her master two and a half years of labor: she will never be able to work enough to pay off the entire debt. Both of them only have grace as their way out! The more important moral of the story regards the relationship between the forgiveness shown the woman and her love for the Master. Unfortunately, some translations render verse 47 as "her sins were forgiven her because she loved much." The original Greek expresses the consequence of the forgiveness she has received: "Her sins were forgiven her in such a way that she loved much." If such a heavy burden of sin had not been forgiven her, she wouldn't have been able to love so much; she is able to love precisely because there are no conditions attached to the grace she has received.

The second part of Jesus' response affirms the primacy of grace: "The one to whom little is forgiven, loves little" (v. 47). This affirmation connects the parable to real life: whoever has not experienced the gratuitous love of God is not in a position to love him.

(Adapted from *The Parables of Mercy*)

… and prayed

Psalm 25:15-18

My eyes are ever upon the LORD,
    who frees my feet from the snare.

Look upon me, have pity on me,
    for I am alone and afflicted.
Relieve the troubles of my heart;
    bring me out of my distress.
Look upon my affliction and suffering;
    take away all my sins.

Psalm 42:2-6

As the deer longs for streams of water,
　　so my soul longs for you, O God.
My soul thirsts for God, the living God.
　　When can I enter and see the face of God?
My tears have been my bread day and night,
　　as they ask me every day, "Where is your God?"
Those times I recall
　　as I pour out my soul,
When I would cross over to the shrine of the Mighty One,
　　to the house of God,
Amid loud cries of thanksgiving,
　　with the multitude keeping festival.
Why are you downcast, my soul;
　　why do you groan within me?
Wait for God, for I shall again praise him,
　　my savior and my God.

Extraordinary Jubilee of Mercy

Rite of the Opening of the Door of Mercy
in Local Churches

December 13, 2015
Third Sunday of Advent

■ ■ ■

The Closing Celebration of the Extraordinary Jubilee
in Local Churches

November 13, 2016
Thirty-Third Sunday of Ordinary Time

Rite of the Opening of the Door of Mercy in Local Churches

December 13, 2015
Third Sunday of Advent

INTRODUCTION

The following *Rite of the Opening of the Door of Mercy in Local Churches* pertains both to the Churches of the Roman Rite and western Churches not of the Roman Rite. The competent authorities of the latter may adjust the ritual to meet local cultural norms.

Bishops of the Eastern Churches, if they wish, may adapt the rite in harmony with their own liturgical traditions.

The day

1. In the bull of indiction *Misericrodiae Vultus* (*MV*), Pope Francis decreed that the Holy Year will begin on the Solemnity of the Immaculate Conception of the Blessed Virgin Mary, December 8, 2015, with the opening of the Holy Door in the Basilica of St. Peter at the Vatican. On the following Sunday, December 13, the Third Sunday of Advent, the opening of the Holy Door of the Cathedral of Rome, the Basilica of St. John Lateran, will take place. After that, the Holy Doors of the other Papal Basilicas will be opened. Moreover, the Holy Father decreed that on the same Sunday, "in every local church, at the cathedral — the mother church of the faithful in any particular area — or, alternatively, at the co-cathedral or another church with special meaning, a Door of Mercy will be opened for the duration of the Holy Year. At the discretion of the local ordinary, a similar door may be opened at any shrine frequented by large groups of pilgrims, since visits to these holy sites are so often grace-filled moments as people discover a path to conversion" (*MV*, 3).

The place

2. The Jubilee Year will be inaugurated in the cathedral of each diocese with the opening of the Door of Mercy at a single celebration of the Liturgy of the Eucharist. If, according to the norms of Canon Law, there is a co-cathedral in the diocese, an opening of the Door of Mercy will also take place there.

Furthermore, a Eucharistic celebration will take place in other churches and shrines in which the diocesan bishop has designated a Door of Mercy. A delegate of the bishop will preside over these ceremonies, at which one of the prayers below is recited at the main door (cf. nos. 40-45).

The nature of the celebration

3. The elements that make up the rite of the opening of the Door of Mercy reflect its character and meaning:

- the mystery of God, rich in mercy and compassion (Eph 2:4 and Jas 5:11), manifested and brought about in Christ, the Father's face of mercy (*MV*, 1), continually at work through the gift of the Holy Spirit (Jn 20:22-23);
- the recognition of Christ as the sole door through which we enter salvation (cf. Jn 10:9) and the one way that leads to the Father (Jn 14:6);
- the Church's ongoing pilgrimage toward "Jesus Christ (who) is the same yesterday, today, and forever" (Heb 13:8).

The celebrant

4. The diocesan bishop presides over the entire ceremony. This accords, on the one hand, with the Lord's Day and the Church's ancient tradition, and, on the other, with the extraordinary event of the Jubilee Year. The Mass of December 13, 2015, will be observed as a stational Mass (cf. *Caeremoniale Episcoporum*, 120) at which the priests, especially the bishop's closest collaborators, concelebrate with him; the deacons, acolytes, and lectors perform their respective ministries, and the lay faithful are encouraged to attend inasmuch as possible.

The specific symbolism of the opening celebration

5. Within the context of the Eucharistic celebration, the specific gesture that marks the beginning of the extraordinary Holy Year is the opening of the Door of Mercy and the solemn procession of the local church — the bishop, clergy, and people — into the cathedral, the Mother Church of all the faithful, where the Pastor of the diocese exercises his magisterial role, celebrates the sacred mysteries, carries out the liturgical acts of praise and supplication, and guides the ecclesial community.

6. This liturgy is composed of five parts:

- the *statio*, either in the church or in another appropriate place,
- the solemn procession,
- the opening of the Door of Mercy and the entrance into the cathedral,
- the renewal of Baptismal promises,
- and the celebration of the Eucharist.

The *statio*

7. The church chosen as the *statio* should be significant and sufficiently large to accommodate those participating in the introductory rites. It should be neither too far from the cathedral nor too close, but rather at a distance conducive to a procession.

8. The constitutive moments of the *statio* are: the greeting and the initial exhortation, the proclamation of a Gospel passage, and the recitation of the opening section of the Bull of Indiction, *Misericordiae Vultus*.

The procession

9. The procession represents the Church's pilgrimage, a practice that "has special place in the Holy Year, because it represents the journey each of us makes in this life" (*MV*, 14). The procession recalls the fact that "mercy is also a goal to reach and requires dedication and sacrifice" (ibid.)

10. Particularly appropriate for the procession are Psalm 86 which resonates with a sense of trust, total abandonment to God, and the hope of his saving help; and Psalm 25 which sings of the goodness of God in whom the Psalmist places his trust and finds serenity and peace. Due to its ancient and multifaceted role in solemn processions, the Litany of the Saints is also very suitable to this occasion.

11. The Book of the Gospels plays an important role in this procession. It should be carried by a deacon. It represents both Christ walking among his people and his Word, the light that guides his disciples.

The opening of the Door of Mercy and the entrance into the cathedral

12. The procession should proceed through the main door of the cathedral, which has particular Christological significance (cf. Jn 10:7,9) and serves as the Door of Mercy, a constant reminder of the meaning of this Extraordinary Jubilee. Using the words of Psalm 118, the bishop invokes the opening of the Door that leads to God's merciful heart made accessible through the open side of Christ on the cross (cf. Jn 19:34). It is in fact the door that leads to salvation as the antiphon based on John 10:9 makes clear. The entrance should therefore be rendered solemn by:

- decorating the door with leafy branches or other ornamentation specific to the local culture, and with fitting Christological symbols;
- by placing special emphasis on the crossing of the threshold: before proceeding inside the cathedral, the bishop should pause together with the entire procession. During this pause, the door itself should be opened and the Book of the Gospels, the word of mercy, should be solemnly displayed, first toward the outside of the cathedral and then toward the inside while the antiphon "I am the door" is sung.

13. Once the pause at the door is completed, the bishop, bearing the Book of the Gospels, moves in procession with the concelebrants toward the altar while the faithful take their places. During this time, the entrance antiphon for the Third Sunday of Advent or some other appropriate hymn is sung.

Renewal of baptismal vows

14. The sacrament of Baptism is the door through which one enters the community of the Church. The rite of blessing the water and sprinkling the community with it is a living reminder of this sacrament. Indeed, Baptism is "the first sacrament of the New Law, through which those who firmly accept Christ in faith and receive the Spirit of adoption become in name and in fact God's adopted children. Joined with Christ in a death and resurrection like his, they become part of his Body. Filled with the anointing of the Spirit, they become God's holy temple and members of the Church, 'a chosen race, a royal priesthood, a holy nation, God's own people'" (*The Book of Blessings*, no. 1080).

The celebration of the Eucharist

15. The celebration of the Eucharist, "as the action of Christ and of the People of God arrayed hierarchically, is the center of the whole Christian life for the Church both universal and local, as well as for each of the faithful individually. For in it is found the high point both of the action by which God sanctifies the world in Christ and of the worship that the human race offers to the Father, adoring him through Christ, the Son of God, in the Holy Spirit" (*The General Instruction of the Roman Missal,* 16). It is precisely for this reason that it stands at the apex of the inaugural celebrations of this Jubilee Year. In the Eucharist, the Father rushes with mercy to meet everyone who seeks God "with a sincere heart," continually offering his covenant to mankind and giving us a foretaste of the eternity of his kingdom, where, we pray, "with the whole of creation, freed from the corruption of sin and death," we may "glorify" the Father for ever (*Eucharistic Prayer IV*).

Things to prepare

16. The following items should be prepared in the sacristy of the stational church:

- the liturgical vestments to be worn by the Bishop, the concelebrating priests, the deacons, and the other ministers at Mass;
- the cope, if the bishop is to wear one during the procession;
- the processional cross and candles;
- the Book of the Gospels;
- the thurible and incense.

These items should be prepared in the cathedral:

- the basin with water to be blessed and used for the sprinkling rite;
- everything necessary for the celebration of Mass (cf. *General Instruction of the Roman Missal,* 117-118).

The Rite of Introduction in the Stational Church

17. On the Third Sunday of Advent, or at First Vespers of that Sunday, at the established time, the faithful gather in a nearby church or another fitting location outside the cathedral (or co-cathedral), toward which the procession will be directed.

18. The Bishop, concelebrating Priests, and Deacons put on violet (or rose) colored liturgical vestments and make their way to where the people are gathered. Instead of a chasuble the Bishop may vest in a cope, which he will remove after the procession.

19. While the Bishop and the ministers go to the places prepared for them, the Hymn of the Jubilee is sung. This hymn may be accompanied by the organ or other suitable instruments.

The Bishop turns to the people and says:

In the name of the Father, and of the Son, and of the Holy Spirit.

The people reply: **Amen.**

He then greets the people with these words:

**The mercy of the Father,
the peace of our Lord Jesus Christ,
and the communion of the Holy Spirit**

be with you all.

The people reply: **And with your spirit.**

20. The Bishop invites the people to bless and praise God:

Cf. Ps 103

**Glory to you, Father, who forgive our faults
and heal our infirmities.**

R. Your mercy endures forever.

**Glory to you, Lord, merciful and kind,
slow to anger and abounding in mercy.**

R. Your mercy endures forever.

**Glory to you, Lord; you who are a
tender Father toward your children.**

R. Your mercy endures forever.

or:

**Blessed are you, Father:
you alone have done great things for us.**   Cf. Ps 136:4

R. Your love endures forever.

**Blessed are you, only begotten Son:
you have freed us from our sins with your blood.**   Cf. Rv 1:5

R. Your love endures forever.

**Blessed are you, Holy Spirit:
consoler of the soul and its most soothing relief.**

Cf. Sequence for Pentecost

R. Your love endures forever.

21. The Bishop then delivers a brief exhortation in these or similar words.

Dearly beloved brothers and sisters,
with eyes fixed on Jesus and his merciful face,
the Holy Father, on the Solemnity of the Immaculate
    Conception,
inaugurated an Extraordinary Jubilee,
thus opening to us and to all men and women
the door of God's mercy.

In communion with the universal Church,
this celebration marks the solemn beginning
of the Holy Year in our diocesan Church;
a prelude to the profound experience of grace and
    reconciliation
that awaits us this year.

We shall joyfully listen to
the Gospel of mercy
that Christ the Lord, the Lamb of God who takes away
    the sins of the world,
continually proclaims throughout the world,
inviting us to rejoice in his love:
a love announced again and again to every creature on earth.

22. After the exhortation, the bishop says the following prayer:

Let us pray.   Cf. Masses for Various Occasions,
                    "For Reconciliation," Opening Prayer, n. 2

O God, author of true freedom,
who desired to gather the whole human race into one
    people,
unshackled from the chains of slavery;

and who give to us, your children, a time of mercy and
  forgiveness;
grant that your Church,
ever expanding in freedom and peace,
may brilliantly shine out to all as a sacrament of salvation;
and make known and active in the world the mystery of
  your love.
We ask this through Christ our Lord.

R. Amen.

23. The proclamation of the Gospel by the deacon follows.

✝ A reading from the Gospel according to Luke   15:1-7

There will be rejoicing in heaven over one sinner who converts

Tax collectors and sinners were all drawing near to listen to
him, but the Pharisees and scribes began to complain, saying,
"This man welcomes sinners and eats with them." So to them he
addressed this parable. "What man among you having a hundred
sheep and losing one of them would not leave the ninety-nine in
the desert and go after the lost one until he finds it? And when he
does find it, he sets it on his shoulders with great joy and, upon his
arrival home, he calls together his friends and neighbors and says
to them, 'Rejoice with me because I have found my lost sheep.' I
tell you, in just the same way there will be more joy in heaven over
one sinner who repents than over ninety-nine righteous people
who have no need of repentance."

The Gospel of the Lord.

24. After the Gospel there may be a short period of silence.
Then a Lector will read the beginning of the Bull of Indiction of
the Extraordinary Jubilee.

From the Bull of Indiction of the Extraordinary Jubilee of Mercy

Misericordiae Vultus (1-3)

Jesus Christ is the face of the Father's mercy. These words might well sum up the mystery of the Christian faith. Mercy has become living and visible in Jesus of Nazareth, reaching its culmination in him. The Father, "rich in mercy" (Eph 2:4), after having revealed his name to Moses as "a God merciful and gracious, slow to anger, and abounding in steadfast love and faithfulness" (Ex 34:6), has never ceased to show, in various ways throughout history, his divine nature. In the "fullness of time" (Gal 4:4), when everything had been arranged according to his plan of salvation, he sent his only Son into the world, born of the Virgin Mary, to reveal his love for us in a definitive way. Whoever sees Jesus sees the Father (cf. Jn 14:9). Jesus of Nazareth, by his words, his actions, and his entire person reveals the mercy of God.

We need constantly to contemplate the mystery of mercy. It is a wellspring of joy, serenity, and peace. Our salvation depends on it. Mercy: the word reveals the very mystery of the Most Holy Trinity. Mercy: the ultimate and supreme act by which God comes to meet us. Mercy: the fundamental law that dwells in the heart of every person who looks sincerely into the eyes of his brothers and sisters on the path of life. Mercy: the bridge that connects God and man, opening our hearts to the hope of being loved forever despite our sinfulness.

At times we are called to gaze even more attentively on mercy so that we may become a more effective sign of the Father's action in our lives. For this reason I have proclaimed an *Extraordinary Jubilee of Mercy* as a special time for the Church, a time when the witness of believers might grow stronger and more effective.

25. After this reading is complete, the Deacon or another minister says the following to begin the procession:

Brothers and sisters,
let us go forth in the name of Christ:
He is the way that leads us
in the year of grace and mercy.

PROCESSION

27. The Bishop places incense in the thurible. The procession to the cathedral (or co-cathedral) where Mass will be celebrated then begins. The thurifer, carrying the lit thurible, goes first, followed by the Deacon carrying the festively decorated processional cross. On each side of him is a candle bearer, followed by the Deacon bearing the Book of the Gospels, then the Bishop, and behind him, the Priests and other ministers, followed by the lay faithful. During the procession, the people and the choir sing the antiphons and psalms proposed below. The Litany of the Saints and other appropriate chants may also be sung.

Antiphon

I will sing of the love of the Lord at all times,
throughout every generation
my mouth shall proclaim his fidelity.   Cf. Ps 89:2

or:

Blessed are the merciful,
for they shall receive mercy.   Mt 5:7

or:

The LORD is good to all,
compassionate to every creature.   Ps 145:9

From Psalm 86

Hear me, LORD, and answer me,
for I am poor and oppressed.
Preserve my life, for I am loyal;
save your servant who trusts in you.

You are my God; pity me, Lord;
to you I call all the day.
Gladden the soul of your servant;
to you, Lord, I lift up my soul.

Lord, you are kind and forgiving,
most loving to all who call on you.
LORD, hear my prayer;
listen to my cry for help.

In this time of trouble I call,
for you will answer me.
None among the gods can equal you, O Lord;
nor can their deeds compare to yours.

All the nations you have made shall come
to bow before you, Lord,
and give honor to your name.
For you are great and do wondrous deeds;
and you alone are God.

Teach me, LORD, your way
that I may walk in your truth,
single-hearted and revering your name.

I will praise you with all my heart,
glorify your name forever, Lord my God.

Your love for me is great;
you have rescued me from the depths of Sheol.

O God, the arrogant have risen against me;
a ruthless band has sought my life;
to you they pay no heed.

But you, Lord, are a merciful and gracious God,
slow to anger, most loving and true.

or:

From Psalm 25

I wait for you, O Lord:
I lift up my soul to my God.
In you I trust; do not let me be disgraced;
do not let my enemies gloat over me.

No one is disgraced who waits for you,
but only those who lightly break faith.
Make known to me your ways, Lord;
teach me your paths.

Guide me in your truth and teach me,
for you are God my savior.
For you I wait all the long day,
because of your goodness, Lord.

Remember your compassion and love, O Lord;
for they are ages old.
Remember no more the sins of my youth;
remember me only in light of your love.

Good and upright is the LORD,
who shows sinners the way,
Guides the humble rightly,
and teaches the humble the way.

All the paths of the LORD are faithful love
toward those who honor his covenant demands.
For the sake of your name, LORD,
pardon my guilt, though it is great.

Who are those who fear the LORD?
God shows them the way to choose.
They live well and prosper,
and his descendants inherit the land.

The counsel of the LORD belongs to the faithful;
the covenant instructs them.
My eyes are ever upon the LORD,
who frees my feet from the snare.

Look upon me, have pity on me,
for I am alone and afflicted.
Relieve the troubles of my heart;
bring me out of my distress.

Put an end to my affliction and suffering;
take away all my sins.
See how many are my enemies,
see how fiercely they hate me.
Preserve my life and rescue me;
do not let me be disgraced, for in trust in you.

ENTRANCE INTO THE CATHEDRAL

28. The procession stops at the main door of the cathedral (or co-cathedral). Here the Bishop says:

Open the gates of justice,
    we shall enter and gives thanks to the Lord.

Cf. Ps 118:19

29. As the door opens, the Bishop says:

This is the Lord's gate:
let us enter through it and obtain mercy and forgiveness.

30. The Deacon gives the Book of the Gospels to the Bishop. Standing at the threshold, the Bishop holds up the Book of the Gospels while the antiphon indicated here (or another appropriate antiphon) is sung. While the Book of the Gospels is shown, the Deacon carrying the processional cross stands directly next to the Bishop.

Antiphon

I am the gate, says the Lord,
    whoever enters through me, will be saved;
    he will enter and go out and find pasture.   Cf. Jn 10:9

31. Once the antiphon is finished, the procession begins again and moves toward the altar: The thurible, cross, and candles go first; the Bishop proceeds next with the Book of the Gospels, followed by the Priests, the other ministers, and the faithful. In the meantime the entrance antiphon or another appropriate antiphon is sung.

Entrance Antiphon   Phil 4:4-5
Rejoice in the Lord always:
    again I say, rejoice,
for the Lord is near!

32. Once the Bishop reaches the altar, he places the Book of the Gospels upon it. Then, if he has worn a cope for the procession, he removes it and puts on a chasuble. He then reverences the altar, incenses it, and finally goes to his chair.

REMEMBRANCE OF BAPTISM AND RENEWAL OF VOWS

33. A container with water to be blessed is brought to the Bishop. The Bishop then invites everyone to pray in these or similar words.

My dear brothers and sisters,
let us ask the Lord to bless this water,
a reminder of our Baptism.
With it, let us invoke the Lord's mercy and salvation
that come through the power of the resurrection of
Jesus Christ.

Everyone prays in silence for a short time.
Then the Bishop continues with hands joined.

Almighty God,

Cf. Roman Missal, Aspersion Rite,
Form 1, second prayer

creator and source of all life,
bless + this water
and grant that we your faithful,
sprinkled from this purifying font,
may receive the forgiveness of sins,
deliverance from all evil,
and the grace of your protection.
In your mercy, O Lord, give us
a spring of living water
springing up to eternal life,
so that, free from every danger,

we may come to you with pure hearts.
Through Christ our Lord.

R. Amen.

34. The Bishop takes the aspergillum and first sprinkles himself, then the concelebrants, then the ministers, and finally the people, walking through the nave of the cathedral (or co-cathedral). While this is taking place, the following antiphons or other appropriate songs are sung.

Antiphon

Cleanse me with hyssop, O Lord, that I may be pure;
wash me, and I will be whiter than snow.   Cf. Ps 51:9

or:

Purify me, O Lord:
and I will be whiter than snow.

or:

I will pour pure water upon you,
and you will be cleansed of every sin,
and I will give you a new heart, says the Lord.

Cf. Ez 47:1-2,9

35. The Bishop then returns to his chair and says:

May almighty God cleanse us of our sins,
and through the celebration of this Eucharist
make us worthy to share at the table of his Kingdom.

R. Amen.

36. The Bishop then sings or says the Collect.

Let us pray.

O God, who see how your people
faithfully await the feast of the Lord's Nativity,
enable us, we pray,
to attain the joys of so great a salvation
and to celebrate them always
with solemn worship and glad rejoicing.
Through our Lord Jesus Christ, your Son,
who lives and reigns with you in the unity of the Holy Spirit,
one God, for ever and ever.

R. Amen.

37. Mass proceeds as usual.

CONCLUDING RITES

38. Before the final solemn blessing, the faithful are to be informed of the churches and shrines in which the bishop has designated a Door of Mercy for gaining a plenary indulgence throughout the Jubilee Year. He then says:

We now turn our thoughts to Mary, the Mother of Mercy.
May her merciful gaze be upon us throughout this Holy Year, so
that all of us may rediscover the joy of God's tenderness.

The assembly then invokes Mary, Mother of Mercy, by singing the *Salve Regina* or the *Alma Redemptoris Mater* or another appropriate song.

The Bishop then imparts the solemn blessing for the season of Advent.

39. After the blessing, the Deacon announces the dismissal as usual. If deemed appropriate, he may say: "Be merciful, just as your heavenly Father is merciful. Go in peace." The people reply: "Thanks be to God." The assembly then goes forth, praising and thanking God.

The Opening of the Jubilee Year in Churches and Shrines Designated by the Diocesan Bishop

40. In the churches and shrines where the bishop has designated a Door of Mercy, the Bishop's delegate, at the appointed time, presides over a Eucharistic liturgy for the Third Sunday of Advent.

At the beginning of the celebration, the celebrant makes his way to the main door of the church or shrine where, after the entrance antiphon has been sung, he begins the celebration with the Sign of the Cross and the greeting as indicated in n. 19. He then invites the congregation to bless and praise the Lord using one of the formulas indicated in n. 20. Once these invocations are finished, he says the following prayer:

> **Let us pray.**
> **Blessed are you, Lord, holy Father,**
> **who sent your Son into the world**
> **to gather all men and women,**
> **wounded and scattered by sin,**
> **into one body through the shedding of his blood.**
>
> **You appointed him both shepherd and gate for the sheep,**
> **so that whoever enters may be saved,**
> **and whoever comes in and goes out**
> **will find pasture for eternal life.**

**Grant that your faithful may pass through this gate,
and be welcomed into your presence,
so that they may experience, O Father, your abundant mercy.
Through Christ our Lord.**

Cf. Book of Blessings, 1229

R. Amen.

41. At the conclusion of this prayer, the celebrant introduces the sprinkling rite with these or similar words:

Dear brothers and sisters, this year of mercy, inaugurated by the Holy Father, invites each of us to a profound experience of grace and reconciliation.
The sprinkling of this holy water is a reminder of our baptism. It recalls the mercy and salvation we have received through the power of Christ's resurrection.

42. After this introduction, the celebrant, accompanied by the ministers, begins to move toward the altar, sprinkling the people with holy water taken from the font at the main entrance. In the meantime, the antiphons indicated in n. 34, or other appropriate songs, are sung.

43. After making a profound bow before the altar and reverencing it with a kiss, the celebrant incenses it and makes his way to the chair where he pronounces the formula indicated in n. 35.

44. The Mass continues as usual with the Collect.

45. At the end of Mass, the assembly may be dismissed with the formula indicated in n. 39.

The Closing Celebration of the Extraordinary Jubilee in Local Churches

November 13, 2016
Thirty-Third Sunday of Ordinary Time

INTRODUCTION

The following directives for the *Closing Celebration of the Extraordinary Jubilee in Local Churches* regards the Churches of the Roman Rite and Churches of other Western, non-Roman rites. The competent authorities of the latter may make changes to adapt the ritual to their particular cultures.

Pastors of Eastern Churches may, if they desire, offer directives in harmony with their own liturgical traditions.

The day

1. In the Bull of Indiction *Misericordiae Vultus*, Pope Francis decreed that the Holy Year would conclude on November 20, 2016, the Solemnity of Our Lord Jesus Christ, King of the Universe, with the closing of the Holy Door in the Basilica of St. Peter's at the Vatican. On the preceding Sunday, November 13, the Thirty-Third Sunday of Ordinary Time, the Jubilee will be brought to a close in local churches.

The place

2. In local Churches, there should be a single celebration of the Eucharist in the cathedral for the closing of the Jubilee Year.

In other churches and shrines that have been designated by the diocesan Bishop as sites of a Door of Mercy, a Eucharistic celebration of thanksgiving should be celebrated, presided over by a delegate of the Bishop.

The celebrant

3. Both the nature of the day and the Church's tradition make it most fitting that the Bishop preside over the entire celebration. Priests, especially his closest collaborators, should concelebrate with the Bishop. Deacons, Acolytes, and Lectors each exercise their respective ministries, and the faithful are strongly encouraged to attend inasmuch as possible. If a closing celebration occurs simultaneously in the co-cathedral, the latter ceremony should be presided over by a delegate of the Bishop.

The celebration of the Eucharist

4. The Mass that concludes the Extraordinary Jubilee is essentially a Sunday celebration of the Eucharist. If the Bishop deems it appropriate, he may use the Mass for Giving Thanks to God, found among the Masses for Various Needs (no. 49) in the Roman Missal. The readings are those assigned to the Thirty-Third Sunday of Ordinary Time, Year C.

Expression of thanksgiving

5. After the Prayer after Communion, the Bishop, in a way harmonious with the liturgical celebration, gives thanks to God for the graces received during the Jubilee Year and invites the assembly to join him in rendering thanks. The Magnificat, insofar as it is the Virgin Mary's song of thanksgiving shared by the Church, is particularly appropriate here.

INTRODUCTORY RITES

6. On the Thirty-Third Sunday of Ordinary Time, at the appointed time, the faithful gather in the cathedral church.

7. Once the people have gathered, the Bishop, concelebrating Priests, and Deacons, vested in green liturgical vestments, begin their entrance procession. The choir and people join in singing the official hymn of the Jubilee Year.

8. The Bishop reverences the altar and proceeds to his chair. He then addresses the assembly in these words.

**In the name of the Father, and of the Son, and of the
    Holy Spirit.**

The people reply: **Amen.**

He then greets the people:

**May the mercy of the Father,
the peace of our Lord Jesus Christ,
and the communion of the Holy Spirit
be with all of you.**

The people reply: **And with your spirit.**

9. The Bishop introduces the assembly to the celebration in these or similar words:

**Dearly beloved brothers and sisters,
we have reached the end of the Jubilee Year.
It has been an extraordinary time of grace and mercy.
In this Eucharistic celebration, we raise our voices to the
Father
in a hymn of praise and thanksgiving**

for all the gifts he has bestowed upon us.
Once more, before approaching these sacred mysteries,
let us invoke the soothing balm of his mercy
acknowledging that we are sinners
and forgiving one another from the bottom of our hearts.

10. After a brief period of silence, the Deacon or another minister says or sings the following invocations:

Cf. Roman Missal, Season of Lent

You command us to forgive one another before approaching your altar: Lord, have mercy.

R. Lord, have mercy.   Or: **Kyrie, eleison.**

You invoked mercy upon sinners as you hung upon the cross: Christ, have mercy.

R. Christ, have mercy.   Or: **Christe, eleison.**

You entrust the ministry of reconciliation to your Church, Lord, have mercy.

R. Lord, have mercy.   Or: **Kyrie, eleison.**

11. The Bishop concludes:

May Almighty God have mercy on us,
forgive us our sins,
and bring us to everlasting life.

R. Amen.

12. The Gloria in excelsis (Glory to God in the highest) is then sung and the Mass continues as usual.

CONCLUDING RITES

13. Following the Prayer after Communion, the bishop invites all those present to thank the Lord for all the spiritual gifts he has bestowed upon them during the Jubilee Year. He may do this in these or similar words:

**Brothers and sisters,
let us joyfully thank God,
the Father of our Lord Jesus Christ.**

**Throughout this year of grace,
he has bestowed on us every heavenly blessing in Christ.
He has given us this precious time
of mercy and conversion.**

**Let us express our thanks and joy
in the words of the Virgin Mary, our Mother.
As we sing the Lord's mercy extending to every generation,
let us ask him to pour out, like the morning dewfall, that
same mercy unceasingly upon the entire world.**

14. The Bishop and people then sing the Magnificat.

15. Once the canticle is finished, the Deacon says:

Bow down for the blessing.

16. Then the Bishop, with hands extended over the people, says the following prayer.   Cf. Roman Missal, Eighteenth Sunday in Ordinary Time, Collect

**Show us your mercy, Lord,
and come to the aid of your people
who call upon you as their shepherd and guide;**

restore what you have created
and keep safe what you have restored.
Through Christ our Lord.

R. Amen.

And may the blessing of almighty God,
the Father, + and the Son, + and the Holy + Spirit,
come down on you and remain with you for ever.

R. Amen.

17. After the blessing, the Deacon announces the dismissal as usual. If deemed appropriate, he may say: "Be merciful, just as your heavenly Father is merciful. Go in peace." The people reply: "Thanks be to God." The assembly then goes forth, praising and thanking God.